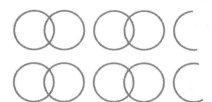

SOLO
SUCCESS!

you **CAN** do things on your own

CH ALL

Solo Success!

First published in 2017 by
Panoma Press Ltd
48 St Vincent Drive, St Albans, Herts, AL1 5SJ, UK
info@panomapress.com
www.panomapress.com

Book layout by Neil Coe.

Printed on acid-free paper from managed forests.

ISBN 978-1-784521-17-2

The right of Christine Ingall to be identified as the author of this work has been asserted in accordance with sections 77 and 78 of the Copyright, Designs and Patents Act 1988.

A CIP catalogue record for this book is available from the British Library.

This book is available online and in bookstores.

Praise for this book

"A MUST for people reluctant to do things alone."

Meryl Van Spall, divorced, retired nurse and college lecturer

"Clear, concise, effective and supportive."

Maria Rooney, divorced, Angelic Reiki and EFT therapist

"Combines perceptive insight with sensible advice."

Michael Hammond, middle-aged and single

*"As a divorced man living alone,
it hit the target with me."*

Angus Clark, fitness instructor

*"This marvellous little book... No nonsense approach,
sensible advice and measurable results."*

Victoria Fraser, widow, retired radiographer

*"The go-to book for solos – it will expand
your life dramatically!"*

Tamar Groeneveld, unmarried, personal fitness and life coach

Dedicated to my mum, Betsy Ingall,
who would have been so proud of me.

Acknowledgements

My thanks, firstly, to my friend Sue Williams, who invited me to take part in an event in 2016 that set me on the journey that has produced this book. That event introduced me to Helen Elizabeth Evans, who eventually asked me the all-important question about my 'expert' subject and to Mindy Gibbins-Klein, 'The Book Midwife', who shared her hard-earned wisdom about the book-writing process.

I am truly grateful for all the encouragement, kind words and constructive feedback from the great mid-lifers who read my draft and helped to make it better. In no particular order: Trudy Box, Michael Hammond, Meryl Van Spall, Victoria Fraser, Adrian Lewis, Tamar Groeneveld, Harulla Ladd, Maria Rooney, Sue Williams, Angus Clark and Jade Sinclair-Milne. Thanks also to Margaret Egrot for sharing her tips on manageable promotion practices.

Finally, thanks, of course, to the support team at Panoma Press.

Preface

A few months ago I was asked to name something on which I considered myself to be an 'expert'. Well, this was autumn 2016 and, as you can imagine, I was naturally cautious to make any such claim, given the apparent mistrust of so-called 'experts' that had surfaced during the Referendum in the summer. So, I have put that word into inverted commas to acknowledge any remaining sensitivities. Anyway, my response at the time was as modest ('I don't consider myself to be an expert in anything') as it was flippant ('unless I can count living on my own'). Apparently I could count living on my own. So, the idea of this book started to take shape.

Why, you might ask, do I think that I am so uniquely qualified to give advice on this subject? As a matter of fact, I am very highly qualified, being single, middle-aged and having lived alone most of my adult life. I therefore have a great deal of experience in overcoming the challenges and fears that accompany the solo lifestyle. More than that, in fact, by managing an active and fulfilled personal life *despite* never having achieved marital status, and *without* a housemate or flatmate or any form of live-in companion to, well, do things with. Together. As a couple or twosome. I have had relationships, of course, and I have a large family and friends with whom I meet regularly to socialise and have fun. We meet to eat out, have coffee, go to the cinema and the theatre and the pub, and enjoy a walk or a class with each other, in twos, threes or a larger group. But I can also do all of those things on my own, quite happily, whenever I want to.

As a member of the single-supplement-paying fraternity, I realise that there are both upsides and downsides to living alone, and my starting point is to take this for granted. However, whilst we should celebrate the upsides, we shouldn't put up with the downsides.

The one thing I won't take for granted is that people without a partner, who live on their own, are somehow second-class citizens, sometimes even *in their own eyes*. I am familiar with, and write about, the fear that makes us single ourselves out (pun intended) of aspects of everyday life, simply because we are not a half of a pair. I therefore hope that my little book will help anyone who struggles with their solo life to live it, doing the things that they enjoy without excuses, and without fear of being seen to be alone.

Contents

Acknowledgements   6

Preface   7

Introduction   10

TAKE RESPONSIBILITY

Chapter 1   Identify your issues   19

Chapter 2   Set some goals   29

Chapter 3   Conquer your fears   43

BE RESOURCEFUL

Chapter 4   Prepare your Action Plan   53

Chapter 5   Activity-related advice   65

              Dining out   65

              Going to the cinema   69

              Going to see a live show performance 71

              Going for a walk   76

Chapter 6   Put the plan into action   83

RESULTS

Chapter 7   Review the event   89

Chapter 8   Celebrate Solo Success!   97

About the Author   102

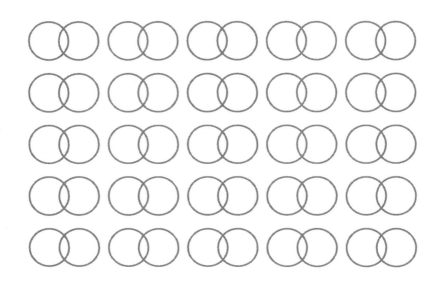

Introduction

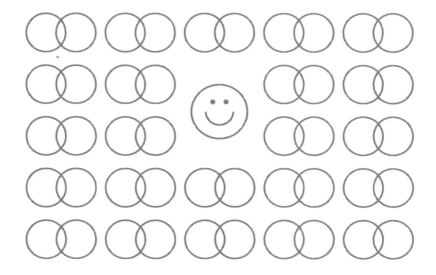

In the UK now, more people than ever before live on their own and the trend is for this to increase even more. Moreover, living alone in mid-life has dramatically increased. Why is this? Three simple facts:

- People are living for longer, and the older you are the more likely you are to live alone.

- Divorce figures are highest for men aged 45 to 49 and for women aged 40 to 44.

- Divorce is the main reason for the increase in living alone for the middle-aged.

There are many advantages to living alone that have been well documented elsewhere, and I won't dwell on them here. It is only natural that some people will embrace their new-found 'freedom' when a relationship ends and, initially at least, will embark on a period of celebration. They are happily solo. However, although they might not miss their former partner, they might miss the *partnership* as demonstrated by the things they did together, or did for each other. The happily solo person might, at some point, feel suddenly alone and dissatisfied with life.

I know from my family, friends, colleagues and acquaintances that middle-aged people can find themselves living alone when a relationship ends for many different reasons. For example, the death of a spouse, or an elderly relative for whom they were the prime carer; an empty nest when children leave home. These people have to face the stark reality of *suddenly* living on their own for the first time in their lives, at a point when they are already suffering and at a loss. These fragile people are not only suddenly living alone but also *reluctantly* solo, and that can, of course, lead to a general dissatisfaction with their life.

I hope that everyone would have family and good friends around to support them at this difficult and challenging time in their life. But family and friends cannot be there all of the time. As a result, in my experience, people who live on their own but are *suddenly and reluctantly* solo find that their social life is restricted *only* to taking part in activities at the invitation of family and friends. They stop doing the things they were used to doing with their partner or significant other person. These can be very normal, everyday, taken for granted activities such as going for a coffee, for a meal out, to the pub, the cinema, the theatre or the local club. These apparently small-scale changes have a large-scale impact over time on people who live on their own. How? They *shrink their lives*. Why? Because of a fear that I have also experienced. The fear of what I call being *visibly alone*.

I believe strongly that everyone should allow themselves to lead the best, positive, productive and happiest life on a daily basis. And I also believe, equally as strongly, that many people who live on their own are not leading that kind of life because they don't know how to, won't allow themselves to, and are afraid to step away from their *shrunken life*.

That's why I have written this book: to help those suddenly living alone, reluctantly solo people, to *expand their shrunken everyday lives* by learning to do things on their own, without someone they know and/or love sitting next to them or across the table. So, if you are one of the increasing millions of people in the UK who is living on your own, at any age but predominantly middle-aged, regardless of status or gender, and you recognise yourself, your circumstances and your attitude in any of the descriptions above, this book is for you!

I would add here that I don't for one minute think that a change to solo status and living alone is necessarily permanent. It can be a transitory phase in your life. Your personal circumstances may well change again in the future. (I have never thought that I would be single and live alone for the rest of my life. I still don't!) But, in the meantime, this little book might help you to live the best, most enjoyable life that you can, through a temporary solo phase.

Similarly, there may be people who are in a relationship who would like to have the courage to pursue hobbies or interests that are not shared by their partner: for example, an evening at a bridge club; practising/learning a martial art; even seeing a film that you know your partner would hate but you would love. The fear of being *visibly alone* is the same for anyone who doesn't have someone by their side when they step into a new environment for the first time.

I have my own experience of changes of circumstances that also meant suddenly being and living on my own in a new environment. Work-related changes in my case threw me into the following:

- A temporary move to a different city (from London to Sheffield) for just over two years.

- A permanent move to a different office location (Coventry) and new home in Leamington Spa.

- Early retirement (stayed put in Leamington Spa).

Big changes in life bring big challenges and, surprisingly, our reaction is to take on more of the same, often because we feel we have no choice. So, while we are busy concentrating on the big stuff happening in our lives – selling, buying and renting property for example – we neglect the little things in life that make all the difference to our wellbeing on a daily basis. That said, how did I respond to the upheaval of suddenly living in a place where I not only had a new job but I also knew hardly anyone at all? I took the standard 'new beginnings' approach, which you will probably recognise from advice about how to meet new people or start afresh in a new town:

- I furthered my adult education: in Sheffield I started an MA; in Leamington I took an Italian class.

- I learned a new skill: in Sheffield I learned to drive and passed my test on the fifth attempt (I was a mature student).

- I followed my passion for singing and joined choirs in both areas.

Fortunately, before any of the above upheavals happened, I had already had some years of solo living and had learned enough by then to make sure that I also enjoyed a social life that didn't rely on or revolve around the new people I had met – on my course, in the choir, or my driving instructor! I could already drink coffee, eat lunch and go to the cinema, the theatre or an exhibition on my own. But the new locations, venues and transport systems, for example, meant that I experienced the feeling, the fear of being *visibly alone* all over again. To overcome the fear, and to get back my confidence, I learned that good planning was more important than ever to make sure that I didn't *shrink my life*.

Over the years I have met many people, both living with a partner and on their own, who have said to me, "Oh it would never occur to me/I couldn't do that/go there on my own!" And my response to them is that, first of all, they appear to be censoring and restricting their own lives. They are not allowing themselves the freedom to choose what they want to do and when they want to do it – regardless of whether anyone else is around to accompany them. I long ago learned not to wait for somebody else to be available in order to, for example, go to see a particular film at the cinema. I wouldn't have seen the film.

It was because of my experience and resourcefulness that when my mum's partner of over 30 years died, Mum sought my 'expert' help. She had moved to a smaller one-bedroomed flat and found herself living alone for the first time in her life. She was in her early seventies, had siblings, children and grandchildren who she saw and spoke to regularly. She met friends in town and went to bingo in the evenings. She was mobile and had all her faculties. But living alone stumped her. She allowed it to *shrink her life*. She telephoned me: "How do I fill my days and evenings? You're the expert on this. What do I do?" I gave her some practical advice, of course, from my own experience. But I realised that Mum was also lonely and missing the regular activities that shaped and filled her daily life with her former partner. One of the things we talked about was perhaps replacing such an activity with something different. For example, just before 4pm each evening, when she would normally have prepared tea for them both, start a crossword or walk into town for a game of bingo instead. In retrospect, I wish I could have given her this book!

Alongside the statistics that show an increase in the number of people living alone, there has been much discussion recently in the press and on broadcast media about an increase in the number of people of all ages who, according to survey reports, have described themselves as 'lonely'. I am of the view that loneliness is a state of mind that is not the preserve of those who live alone. On the contrary, people can feel lonely at any age, in a crowd, in a room full of people they know and, indeed, in a relationship. This book isn't about dealing with loneliness per se, or the changes/triggers that might be considered a cause of feelings of loneliness, such as divorce or bereavement. But if you live on your own and feel lonely, I hope that this book will help you to find ways to cope better and perhaps even to overcome that feeling.

Now, I have some questions for you. Are you ready to change your solo life for the better? Are you ready to *expand your solo life*? Do you want to learn to love your life? Your *solo* life?

If the answer is YES then I can help you. The truth is that change is difficult but people do it all the time. So **you** can do it. To *expand your life* I will show you how to:

- Take responsibility for your own everyday life and plan to change it.

- Conquer the main fear that stops you doing things on your own.

- Successfully undertake activities on your own.

- Respect yourself and your needs more.

- Become a Solo Success!

On that point about respecting yourself, throughout the next chapters I will include short **Self-respect** sections that remind you of the importance of self-worth and self-love in supporting self-belief. If you want to make changes in your life, you need to believe that your happiness is important. Believe that you are worth some personal investment, time and effort. That **you are worth it** and that **you deserve it**. It is very important to show yourself respect by taking care of yourself holistically, in mind, body and spirit. As you start to and succeed in doing more and more activities on your own, your confidence and overall wellbeing will improve more and more. So, if you also take some time during your change process to work on your general wellbeing, you will develop a mutually supportive internal system that is all about making you feel good.

All my experiences during some 30 years of living continuously on my own are distilled into the advice and tips in this book. If you follow that advice, if only to change one thing, I can guarantee that you will have new, good experiences – and you will want to keep having them!

I guarantee that you will discard your *shrunken live-alone life* to become a Solo Success who can enjoy doing things on your own!

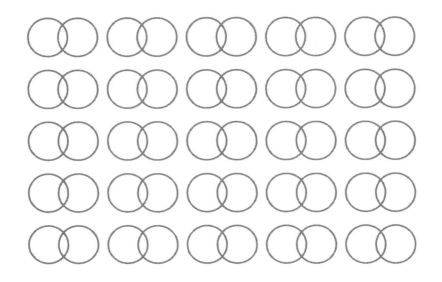

TAKE
RESPONSIBILITY

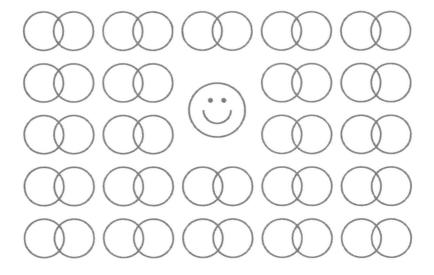

CHAPTER 1

Identify your issues

Well done! You are still here. You have taken the first step on your journey to Solo Success! So, let's get started.

The first thing that you need to acknowledge to yourself is that you are in charge of your own life. You are in control. You always have been ever since you became a decision maker about your present and future life. Now think about this: at some point, or at many points, while living alone, you made a decision, or many small decisions, to *shrink your life*. What? When? How? Let's look at this logically.

Think about some of the decisions that you have made in the past. Try and identify actual decisions that you have made in your past – good and bad – that had an impact on your life. I'm talking about big decisions, for example to:

- Go to university abroad.

- Take a job straight out of school rather than go to university.

- Take a gap year and travel the world for experience/to work for a charity.

- Sell the family home.

- Pursue promotion at all costs.

Other people will, at times, have influenced or made decisions that impacted on you and decisions you have made. But let's not get into blaming other people – just look at the decisions *you* have made.

Now, if you have identified some bad decisions, and we have all made them, think about why you remember them, perhaps very easily. I suspect that, if you are honest, you will have identified more bad than good decisions. Am I right? And the reason that you remember these decisions is because you learned a valuable lesson from them. We learn best from the mistakes we make in life. Take a minute or two to think about the lessons *you* learned from the mistakes *you* made. This isn't a beating yourself up exercise. Far from it! Treat it as a celebration of the positive things that you have learned and that changed your life for the better. And all arising from the mistakes to which you bravely and willingly admit!

So, earlier, I challenged you with the assertion that you must have made at least one decision, if not more, that *shrank your life* when you started living on your own. These decisions will have started life as soft and slippery thoughts that ultimately resulted in you not doing the things that you took for granted. These thoughts are always fighting to get the best space in your head and will triumph if you let them.

Importantly, all these little negative decisions (I won't do that, I won't go there) came up in your brain with stealth and cunning, gradually, insidiously. And where is the evidence for this? **You** have the evidence! At various moments, over a period of time that only you can identify and determine, **You** made decisions to stop doing certain things. These were things that you would otherwise enjoy doing with someone else but you felt that you couldn't or didn't want to do them on your own. Can you admit to any such things? This is difficult stuff. Think about it over a few days if you have to. Come back to it after thinking about the insidious, pernicious negativity that *shrank your life*. And think about whether you want to change your life for the better now that you are on your own.

Or don't wait. Do something now. Whenever you decide to do this, you can start to take some stock. Take some responsible action that will move you forward. I suggest that you make a list of three or four everyday activities that you like doing but that you have always thought of as something you can only do with other people or another person/friend. This list might include some of the following:

- Going to the cinema/theatre/a concert.

- Going to a sporting event – cricket, football or athletics.

- Going for a walk.

- Calling into a pub /bar/café for a drink or a snack.

I cannot emphasise enough at this stage that I am only concerned with activities that constitute a part of everyday life. I am not asking you to list your heart's desires, your bucket list of places to see before you die, or the three wishes you would ask a genie to grant. This is not about big dreams. I am only asking you to come up with a list of things, such as those on the list above, that would make a difference to your quality of life if only you could bring yourself to do them on your own.

SELF-RESPECT 1

All behaviour is learned. We have all learned as a result of our experiences what types of behaviour are considered normal in society. Thankfully it is increasingly rare in today's civilised western society for anyone – even a woman – to be dealt with awkwardly or regarded suspiciously for having a drink in a bar or café, or going to an event on their own. So never undervalue or behave apologetically about, or have low expectations of, any activity you undertake on your own. If you do, you not only allow society to undervalue you as a customer and participant but you will also find that your experience will always fall short. It will match your low expectations.

You have every right to be there on your own.

Value this and the activity and you will value your self-worth.

Think about the last time you did any of the activities on your list, on your own. Be honest – have you ever done any of these things on your own? If you have and you are confident about that as a solo activity, it shouldn't be on your list. Your list should be specific to you and your interests and lifestyle.

For my part, my list of 30 years ago would have included most of the list on the previous page. But my greatest fear was definitely eating out alone. I remember that even at university I hated having to walk into the refectory at lunch or dinner times *on my own*. I dreaded walking between rows of happily chatting groups of friends – some of them my friends – looking for a space on a table, desperate for someone I knew to hail me and invite me to join their group. It was torture. It wasn't until I was forced through my job to stay overnight in a hotel or B&B on my own that I started to overcome the fear of walking into the hotel or B&B restaurant. Or if there wasn't one, or it was too late for it to be open when I arrived, a local pub down the road. I still shiver at the recollection of walking into a pub in a small Yorkshire town, just to get something to eat, and the entire male clientele at the bar turning as one to stare at me in disbelief. But that was in the 1970s and my experiences then helped me to overcome my fear and develop the simple strategies that I will share with you.

You might also want to consider including personal stuff that relates to your specific interests and hobbies. Crucially, this list might also include things that you *didn't* do when you were in a relationship/living with someone else. Only you know what these might be. The important thing is that it is the right list for you.

When a long-term relationship ended, I was determined to pursue something that I felt I was influenced *to not do* by my former partner. I was (am!) a good singer and through a work colleague I was given the opportunity to audition for and perhaps join a choir. The regular meetings and rehearsals were on a Friday night, close to where we worked in the centre of London. My partner was happy for me to go once to try it out but when I said that I really enjoyed it and wanted to join, he was not supportive of me having a regular commitment on a Friday night. That was a night when we regularly saw each other and the start of our weekend together. Those regular plans would need to change if I was going to be in a choir rehearsal every Friday night. Anyway, I listened to him. I let him influence me. I didn't join that particular choir but I've joined many since then, regardless of whether I was in a relationship.

What will be on your list? What are your equivalents of my fear of eating alone in public? Or not following a route that would support and nurture a hobby or other interest? Take your time and make sure that your list of things that you want to be able to do on your own is your honest list. But don't get side-tracked by big dreams or wish-lists. Your list should not be about, for example, swimming with dolphins or going on safari. That is a different kind of list altogether.

You can take a few hours, a few days or weeks to refine it but never waver from the intention of making a list. What is really important is that you capture the real things that you want to be able to do, in some detail, in order to feed into your Plan – the next stage in your progress to Solo Success. However many things you have on your list – one or 40 – we are going to deal with them.

So, you've got your list – bravo! Now you have to get through the next stage before you can start to tackle your list. I'd like you to take part in an exercise – the first of four exercises, if you are up for them. You will need the list of things that you want to be able to do on your own, including anything that is to do with a hobby, interest or passion that you haven't been brave enough to start to pursue before, or have felt that you were prevented in pursuing.

EXERCISE 1

In this exercise I am going to ask you to do some honest self-analysis – and I mean honest! It is essential to be honest with yourself. So, make that decision – a good decision – right now. Well done and thank you!

Firstly, you need to identify three or four main reasons why you stopped yourself from doing something that you would have to do on your own. The activities that are on your list.

Exercise continued

What are the fears that are making you *shrink your life*? Why are you stopping yourself from doing what you want to do/having some fun?

To do this properly and seriously, allocate some special time for yourself, alone. Make sure that you will have no distractions. So turn off your mobile phone or put it on aeroplane mode. Make yourself comfortable, perhaps by lying down or sitting in your favourite chair. Dim the lights, light a fragrant candle or joss stick and put on some gentle music. Put yourself in the mood for only concentrating on the fears that are stopping you from living a full life on your own. Take as long as you need. You've got some free time? This will not only help you to fill it usefully, it could change your life!

It will help if you concentrate on specific events and why you didn't go ahead simply because you would have to do it on your own. For example: you were hungry but you walked past your favourite restaurant; you wanted to see a special one-night-only cinema screening but your friends didn't like the late start; your favourite comedian was appearing at a venue in a nearby town but no one else you know was interested.

By the way, feel free to add any activity to a list at any stage in a process. We don't always get it right first time and can continue to change and refine and reprioritise throughout. In fact, I hope you will. That way we will get to the heart of what you really want to change/do better/do more/do differently and, moreover, do on your own.

Back to your fears. Is it that you fear:

- Panic, for example, at not knowing what to do/how to behave and doing the wrong thing?

Exercise continued

- Embarrassment at making a fool of yourself?

- Feeling or looking stupid?

- Not knowing what to say or how to behave?

- Drawing unwanted attention to yourself?

- Being seen to be on your own?

- All of the above?

- Something else?

Some or all of these fears may be the same things that have stopped you from doing things all your life. Do you recognise them? Other people may have brought one or more to your attention in a helpful or, let's face it much more likely, unhelpful way. They are all valid fears – and they can be overcome! Trust me. And believe me, the very first step in overcoming any fear is to acknowledge it.

So, once you have honestly acknowledged and written down your absolute fear or fears, you can put this/these alongside your list of things/activities that you want to be able to do on your own. Then we can start to set some goals to help you to move forward in achieving what you want to do, and that take account of your fears.

SELF-RESPECT 2

As a reward for completing this first exercise, organise a special night in on your own to celebrate. Set a date with yourself, for example a weekday night that wouldn't normally be out of the ordinary. Organise something that you consider to be a treat. You could watch a box set of a favourite show that you haven't got round to; start to read a novel that you bought months ago; pamper yourself with hair/facial treatments, or a home manicure/pedicure; soak in the bath; cook a recipe that you have wanted to try and buy wine to go with it.

Remember – you are worthy.

By valuing your achievements you are valuing yourself.

CHAPTER 2

Set some goals

If you are serious about tackling the issues and being able to do the things you have identified, the next active step you need to take is to set some goals, or objectives. These will be specific to what you want to achieve and they will be SMART to give you focus and clarity. By SMART I mean:

S	=	specific
M	=	measurable
A	=	achievable
R	=	realistic
T	=	time limited

The table below gives some more information on what each of those headings means. You will need your list of things you want to do to relate to each element of the table.

SPECIFIC	Be as specific in describing what you want to do as possible. For example, 'join a gym' is better than 'join some sort of sports club'; 'go to a salsa class' is better than 'go dancing.'
MEASURABLE	How will you know you have achieved your objective? This reminds you to include an element of measurability in your objective eg 'in the next month'; 'starting on Sunday'.
ACHIEVABLE	Don't be too ambitious. Be kind to yourself. You might realise that a specific goal needs to be broken down into smaller goals. You can't climb Mount Kilimanjaro next Thursday and you will need many supporting goals to achieve that, even by next year!
REALISTIC	This sits alongside both ACHIEVABLE and TIME LIMITED. This reminds you to take into account all your existing responsibilities. When will your diary be free for you to include something new? How much time will the activity take daily/weekly/ monthly? How much research/preparation time do you need?
TIME LIMITED	This is about the end date for the achievement of your goal. You will need to take all the other elements into account in order to set this. If possible, set goals, initially, that you can achieve by the end of the next two months.

I realise that you might feel a bit daunted by goal setting if you have to try and meet all the above criteria. But these are to help you to be clear about exactly **what** you want to do and **by when** you want to achieve it. Don't forget also that one goal might be the stepping stone to another: you can't achieve goal B before you have achieved goal A! Don't worry, I will help you by giving you some tips and worked examples.

The first tip I am going to give you is that it is easier to look at the criteria with the initial letters in a different order from that given in the acronym above. So, let's work through some of the types of activities that you may have on your list.

To go to something – for example the cinema, theatre, a comedy club, a spectator sports match/game – *on your own*.

SPECIFIC	Is there a specific venue that you can name and/or film, play, artist, musician, sports event to identify?
TIME LIMITED	When do you want to do this by? Do you need to take into account dates and programmes for your chosen event?
REALISTIC	Does your event require tickets that need to be bought well in advance? Will you realistically be able to get a ticket?
ACHIEVABLE	Looking at the event, date it takes place and ticket availability, will you be able to achieve this by your chosen date?
MEASURABLE	Finally, do you know how you will be able to measure that you have achieved it? Will it be obvious because your date for achievement is specific, realistic and achievable?

Here are a few examples of SMART and non-SMART goals.

SMART	NON-SMART
I will go and see the new James Bond film on the first Saturday of showing at my local cinema [insert name if applicable] when it opens in June.	I want to see the next new James Bond film.
I will go to a performance of the next play at [name of local theatre] before the current programme ends in June.	I want to see a show at [name of local theatre] in the next season.
I will attend a home [name of ground] cricket match during the county championship in July.	I want to attend a [name of ground] County cricket match this summer.

Can you see the difference between the SMART and the non-SMART goals? How vague the non-SMART goals are compared with the more specific SMART variety? How you would be able to measure the achievement of the SMART goals more easily?

The other important thing to notice is that all the SMART goals begin with 'I will'. This is a significant change to help you to form a real intention to do something. You are more likely to do something that you say you *will do* as opposed to *want to do*.

Where you have gaps that need to be filled around venues, ticket prices and availability, programme listings etc. you will need to undertake some more research to SMART-en up your goals. Nowadays, you can find out everything you need to know about any organisation, and its main business, from its website. So, go online to fill in all those gaps that you will have identified while formulating your SMART goals above. Here's a non-exhaustive list of the sort of detail that you can find on specific organisation websites that will help to get you started:

- Cinema/theatre programme listings: show start and finish times, ticket prices and availability, how to book tickets, membership costs and advantages, for example special offers, details of special events.

- College course listings: descriptions, availability, eligibility and costs by term/year.

- Voluntary organisation membership: volunteer requirement details and application forms.

- Restaurants/cafés/pubs: opening and closing times, example menus and costs, specific festive menus and costs, special offers/deals, booking a table online.

- In most cases for all above: directions, access for the disabled, car parking.

The internet is a real godsend. Back in the day when I realised that I was becoming a summer cricket widow, I set myself a goal to see a theatre performance in London's West End every Saturday during what remained of the cricket season. This was in the early to mid-1980s – before the World Wide Web or even the availability of personal computers. So my research, had it been at theatre level, would have started with the weekly theatre listings published in the *London Evening Standard* and the weekend broadsheets. Next, a relentless slog around or phone calls to various West End theatres, noting show times and prices etc. However, I took an easier and cheaper route by queuing at the Leicester Square half-price ticket booth (as it was then) and taking pot luck on the shows for which tickets were available.

If you have any goals that are similar to the ones in this section, try drafting a few SMART goals for yourself. And remember to start each one with 'I will...' or you can move on to more examples below.

To join something – for example a gym, a local club, a choir, an evening class.

SPECIFIC	Do you have more than one choice of gym, choir etc? Or do you know exactly which one you want to join? Do you know where you might be able to take up your choice of class? Or do you need to look at a course prospectus?
TIME LIMITED	When do you want to achieve this by? Are there any specific enrolment/joining times for new people? Is there a process that will take some time, eg application/auditions/trials?
REALISTIC	Do you meet all (if any) membership or eligibility criteria? Do you know the cost of membership? Can you afford it?
ACHIEVABLE	Once you know what you might have to do and how long this might take, do you need to look again at your deadline?
MEASURABLE	Will you be able to measure that you have achieved it?

Here are a few more examples of SMART and non-SMART goals for the above.

SMART	NON-SMART
I will join my local gym [name if possible] on the 1st of the next month and attend at least twice a week for the next three months.	I want to join a local gym and get started by Christmas.
I will audition for the [name of specific choir] in June so that I can attend the required number of rehearsals to sing in the Christmas concert.	I want to sing in the [name of choir] Christmas concert this year.
I will enrol on [name of college] Italian conversation class in time to start in the autumn term.	I want to go to an Italian conversation class next term.

You will notice that there are some complications around joining a group or organisation to do with, for example, choices, membership criteria, enrolment times and fees. These are also things that you will need to research. But in the meantime, where you don't have some of this information you can leave gaps to fill in later. Taking the second of the three SMART goals above, it might instead state: I will audition for the [name of specific choir] in [the appropriate month] so that I can attend... etc. Try writing some of these types of SMART goals with the appropriate gaps that might need to be filled in later. The important thing is that you are starting to put down in writing the first steps to achieving something that will *expand your life* again.

SELF-RESPECT 3

People talk about being 'fit for life' and I'm sure we all aspire to achieve that for ourselves. You are actively planning for and undertaking changes in your lifestyle and need to look after yourself physically. So, are you fit for the life you want to lead in the future? Your Solo Success-full life? We have all learned that it is sensible to reduce our intake of salt, sugar and starchy carbohydrates (bread, potatoes and pasta) to better look after our blood pressure, cholesterol levels and, especially, our hearts. If you haven't had these three vital checks for some time, or you are worried about your general health in any way, make an appointment to see your GP for a check-up.

By valuing your health, and wanting to improve it, you are valuing yourself.

Going into a café, pub or restaurant to have a drink or a meal; and also going for a walk.

These activities are generally perceived by those who live on their own to be the preserve of the couple or to be group oriented. They are, therefore, also generally perceived to be the most difficult to undertake alone.

SPECIFIC	Is there a specific venue that you can name? Or an event at a venue nearby or known to you? A specific day and /or time of day that is preferable?
TIME LIMITED	When do you want to start doing this? What do you need to take into account that might affect this date?
REALISTIC	What needs must be met before you can start to achieve this?
ACHIEVABLE	Are there any other factors that might prevent you being able to achieve this by your chosen date?
MEASURABLE	Will you be able to measure that you have achieved it? Will it be obvious because your date for achievement is specific, realistic and achievable?

In my experience, these types of activity goals are the sort that you can decide to go and do there and then, after taking a deep breath and without any plan or preparation. So, bravo if that is what you think is best for you! However, if this wouldn't be your approach, you might like to consider some preparation to ensure that you feel comfortable and confident and, importantly, that the activity fits into your life and the way you lead it. My advice on how you might do this is covered in Chapters 4 and 5, but in the meantime, let's look at some potential SMART and non-SMART goals.

SMART	NON-SMART
From [enter day/date eg next Thursday] I will walk to and back from [name of place that you go to] on [day that you go there] and take in the local park or riverside walk each time.	Every time I go to [name of place] I'll park at [name of place] and go and have a little walk.
From [enter date] I will go to [my favourite or name of café] for coffee and/or lunch after I have finished [name activity eg shopping/teaching/volunteering at...].	I want to go to that really buzzing coffee shop on the corner of the street after I've finished my shift at [name of place.]
Next [enter day] when I am coming back from [enter place or activity] and it is after 7pm when I get to [name pub/restaurant] I will stop there and have dinner.	If it's not too late when I next pass [enter pub/restaurant] on my way back from [enter place/activity] I will stop and have something to eat.

The most obvious thing to point out here is that I have given a 'from' start date. I think it helps with this kind of goal that you envisage the new activity as part of a day or time of day that you would usually also do something else, such as a regular activity or commitment. You are adding to, therefore expanding, this normal day. Thinking of the new activity in this way will make it easier for you to select a future start date! Of course, there is no reason why these sorts of activities shouldn't be brand new and stand-alone, on a day that you are normally free. In either case you will still need a 'start from' date.

Notice where the differences between the SMART and non-SMART goals are stark and where they are more subtle and in which different aspects. Check what is missing from the non-SMART goals. Which of them is/is not specific, measurable, achievable, realistic or time limited enough?

OK, there's been a lot to absorb in this section but before we move on to the next chapter, which is all about **how** you are going to set about achieving your goals, there is another exercise to do. Have a go at it before moving on as you will appreciate the effort when you come to formulating a Plan later on.

EXERCISE 2

Despite having fears that you haven't conquered, and goals that are not SMART enough (probably), please trust me. Forget all your fears – for the moment. I will tell you how to deal with them. Don't worry that your first attempt at goals looked more like the ones in the non-SMART column. You can improve them. That's exactly what you are going to do now.

Taking your original list of activities that you want to be able to do on your own, and the goals that you have written and re-written, I invite you now to rewrite your goals as the best SMART goals that you can. Take into account these four key points:

1. Start with, or include, the intention 'I will...'

2. Following any research as above, fill in any gaps in detail.

   Or

3. Put in gaps for the unknown details that you can insert following some research using the bracket [...] technique that I have employed above. Keep a list/note of what the gaps are that you need to fill. If you don't fill those gaps with the required information now, you will need to do it in the next section.

4. Try to set goals that fit into/around and take account of your current life and responsibilities. If that is not possible, because your current life and responsibilities need to change, then you have a whole new set of goals to achieve that will make possible the goals that you are considering!

It is also important to remember not to be over-ambitious. You are taking active steps to change your life for the better. And they can be small steps, at least to start with.

One of the ways to prepare mentally and to signal to your brain that you are starting a change process (effectively telling your brain to stand by and get ready) is to make a small change to a regular routine. We all love our routines but they are just habitual behaviours which can sometimes tell us that we have got into a rut, become a bit staid. So, surprise yourself by changing one of those routines. I'm not asking you to stop doing something altogether but just to think about when, where or how you might do something. For example, for some time I used to listen to *The Archers* on the radio every night when I got home from work. If I missed an episode because I didn't get home in time, I became grumpy. So, I put a stop to the regular evening routine and started to listen to the Sunday morning omnibus edition instead. Nowadays, I don't have to worry if I miss that as I can catch up whenever I want to on the BBC iPlayer.

Some of the small routine changes that you could make include:

- The route you drive/walk to the shops or work;

- The day or time that you do a big supermarket shop;

- Shopping online rather than in person;

- What you eat for breakfast;

- The time that you go to bed or get up in the morning;

- Having only a Sunday rather than daily newspapers;

- The time of day and where you do a crossword or other puzzle.

You will start to notice how easy a small change is to make, and how different you feel, in a positive way, if you just change one regular routine. And this small success will start to build up your confidence to tackle the new challenges ahead.

SELF-RESPECT 4

One place where you might find you can make some changes is in your home environment. Is your house/flat a cosy nest or is it a messy shambles where you can't find anything? Is it worthy of you and supporting your values and goals? In your view, is there room for improvement in any of your rooms?

Any decorating, minor repairs, a set of shelves, de-cluttering or just moving furniture around required? Changes to your surroundings have an amazing impact on your brain (opening up to/preparing for change) and your outlook. You don't need to spend a lot of money. In the first flat I owned, my sitting room furniture was second-hand and from junk shops. I decided to paint it all black (trendy at the time) in an attempt to create a more coherent look. I was thrilled with the chic and stylish end result, for little money, time and effort.

Value yourself by valuing your space.

CHAPTER 3

Conquer your fears

In the previous chapter I acknowledged that you will still have fears about doing an activity on your own. These will be the fears that you listed in the first chapter about taking responsibility. See, I haven't forgotten! Take a look at your list now and keep it by you through this next section. It may look like the list I gave you, copied again for you here:

- Panic, for example, at not knowing what to do/how to behave and doing the wrong thing?

- Embarrassment at making a fool of yourself?

- Feeling or looking stupid?

- Not knowing what to say or how to behave?

- Drawing unwanted attention to yourself?

- Being seen to be on your own?

- All of the above?

- Something else?

In my experience, the biggest fear that we all have to face is the one that I have hidden in the list, third from the bottom: that of being seen to be on your own. I have already referred to this as being *visibly alone*. So, let's tackle this one now and once and for all. It is this most crippling of fears that will impact the most on where, when and how you decide to carry out the activity to meet your goal. Let me help you to set your parameters so that you can alleviate this fear.

Firstly, it is only *your perception* that everyone else around you sees or notices you and has a sudden insight into your personal circumstances so that they can say with certainty, 'He/she is on their own.' And, let's get this straight, there is no sign hovering above your head, or hanging around your neck, that everyone else can read, that declares 'I'm on my own!'. Unless you are planning on wearing such a sign, you can assume that no one immediately knows and, importantly, judges your solo status.

You might perceive that your body language and behaviour could indicate that you are on your own, if you allow it, in the same way as if you are wearing a sign such as mentioned above. But again, this is *your perception* of what everyone else is seeing and thinking. With experience, and by following my tips, you will grow in confidence so that you don't particularly notice the other people around you or worry about what they might be thinking about you.

I realise and can understand that, at least initially, you may not be able to face the prospect of being anywhere where people might know or recognise you, because you really don't want to discuss your current situation. If you are attending an event or undertaking an activity in a place where people might know you and your circumstances, you could very well perceive yourself to be *visibly alone* more easily to some specific people.

In circumstances where you want to avoid people, you might want to choose to strike out on your own in a place where you have less risk of bumping into someone you know. Perhaps choose a nearby town or city that you know quite well. By wearing the cloak of anonymity the more invisible you will become, or rather you will perceive yourself to be. However, before rushing to choose such a place, remember that you are trying to make changes that will impact on your life for the better, and also will fit in with your current lifestyle. Do you really want to have to go to another town just to see a film or have a coffee?

There may well be some things that you would more easily and more appropriately be able to try for the first time on your own, outside your home location. For example, a fan-based attraction/event, such as the *Strictly Come Dancing* tour, a championship boxing match, a touring production of a favourite musical or an athletics tournament. It is worth considering that even if you go on your own to such an event, the people sitting on either side of you will also be fans/enthusiasts. So, you will have something in common with them and something to talk about. My advice would be to consider the location for each specific goal, if you need to, and take into account my other tips for your chosen activity in Chapter 5.

With experience, you will learn to respond to and behave with confidence around other people when you are out alone. Bear in mind that total strangers are more likely to be friendly than not! And if you are out and about on your own and see people who you know, whether well or merely as acquaintances, they might ask you to join them. Just as when you had been with a partner or a group of family or friends, you are free to choose whether or not you accept such an invitation. You can be spontaneous about whether you join a group or remain solo!

Most importantly, don't be afraid to say to people who ask about who you are with that you are on your own. Whoa, I can hear you say! Hang on a minute... isn't that going a bit far?! I realise that you might have to practise saying out loud to someone, 'Actually, I'm here on my own' or words to that effect – so practise if you need to. But by telling someone that you are alone you are not only being honest – to them and to yourself – you are also helping to dispel your real concerns about how other people might be perceiving and/or judging you. It is as good as throwing away the imaginary sign hovering over your head or hanging around your neck.

EXERCISE 3

Look at the list of fears/issues that are preventing you from (at the moment) undertaking the activity around which you have built your goal. How many of these fears are to do with your own perception of how other people might see you and judge you? I'm guessing most if not all. And how much worse would making a fool of/ embarrassing yourself or generally being socially inept be if, to top it all, you are also, in your view, *visibly alone*? So, let's try and do something about this whopper of fears.

Imagine that you are walking into the place/venue that you want to go into on your own. You are wearing a helmet that holds a large, flashing, brightly lit sign of an arrow bearing the words ON MY OWN! This attracts attention to you and people start to react as you move through the crowd. They are laughing, sniggering and turning away from you. This is exactly what you have feared! How does this make you feel? How do you react to their cruelty? Now, see yourself going outside the building and taking off the helmet as you walk away. You are determined, resolved never to wear that stupid helmet again. Say this out loud: 'I will never, ever wear that

Exercise continued

stupid helmet again!' Say it a few more times and make sure that you mean it. Finally, see yourself throwing the helmet away in a roadside skip. What are the new emotions that you feel? Relief? Surprise? Joy? Take a few moments to really enjoy the positive emotions that you feel.

Finally, write down that sentence: 'I will never, ever wear that stupid helmet again!' Copy it out a number of times on slips of paper that you can put into your coat pockets, your favourite or most used bag, or in the well of your car dashboard – places where you can access it and look at it quickly and easily. Reach for and read that sentence whenever you feel the fear of walking into a space because of your perception of being *visibly alone* in the future. This will remind you that you no longer wear the helmet and the sign. You threw it away and, along with it, your fear.

SELF-RESPECT 5

Millions of people the world over these days practise mindfulness, a therapeutic mental technique with its roots in Buddhist meditation. Research has proven that mindfulness practice shrinks the brain's fight or flight centre, the amygdala. This part of the brain is involved in the initiation of the body's response to stress – destructive emotions such as fear, anxiety, anger and unhappiness.

The formal practice of mindfulness is commonly referred to as meditation. There are many ways in which it can be practised alone and in groups.

A common form of practice that has developed this century is through guided meditation via an internet application, such as Headspace. Meditation apps are available from App Stores and many come with a free trial period, which is a good way to get started.

Value yourself by improving how you deal with stress.

Strengthen Your Resolve

To achieve your goal you will need to have a strong and positive mental attitude. This doesn't mean concentrating on your goal at the expense of everything else. No – far from it! It means building achievement of your goals into your everyday life so that it becomes second nature to you. You can do this by:

- Reminding yourself every day of your goal and why you are pursuing it in order to build up positive energy around it.

You can build this into your daily routine, perhaps at the same time every day. For example, first thing in the morning while brushing your teeth; on your journey to the shops/ work; last thing at night before going to sleep. Ask yourself and answer these questions, speaking out loud if possible:

- What am I aiming to achieve?

- Why do I want to achieve this?

- Why haven't I done this before?

- How much better will I feel about myself once I have achieved this?

• Put little written reminders of, or pictures representing, your goal around your home such as on post-it notes or postcards stuck to the fridge or the back of a door – anywhere that you will regularly see them!

• The average person has around 70,000 thoughts a day, most of them negative or self-critical, according to a character in the TV drama *Cold Feet*. Tell the negative voices inside your head to SHUT UP! Respond with a positive assertion, perhaps a little mantra that you use on each occasion. For example, every time you hear a little voice doubting your ability to bring something new into your life that you can do on your own, just say: 'Be quiet! I know I can and I will achieve my goal to [insert]. '

Whether you start doing just one or all of these positive actions, you will be surprised at how quickly you start to make them regular practices, and what a difference they make to your attitude and willpower. You should gradually start to feel more confident and in control. And don't worry if you experience a blip, a momentary lack of confidence or forgetting/failing to run through a regular routine or mantra. That is to be expected whenever we start to try and effect a change in our lives. Just start afresh the next day.

Once you have made these positive actions part of your regular daily routine, and practised the exercise to help you to conquer your fear of being *visibly alone*, don't stop doing them once you have decided that you are ready to prepare your Action Plan. Because, believe it or not, it is through the preparation and undertaking of your Action Plan that you will continue to build up and maintain the confidence to ultimately see your Plan through to achievement. By preparing yourself mentally, physically and emotionally as you build the steps of your Action Plan, you are continuously improving your chances of success. Think how many days of Action Planning God metaphorically needed to put in place the building blocks to achieve the grand finale of Creation! So, turn to the next chapter and let's get started.

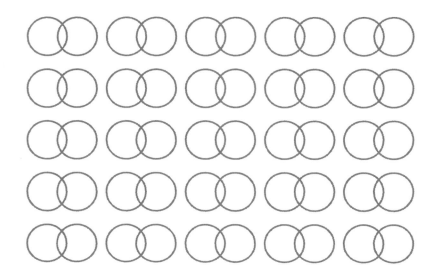

BE
RESOURCEFUL

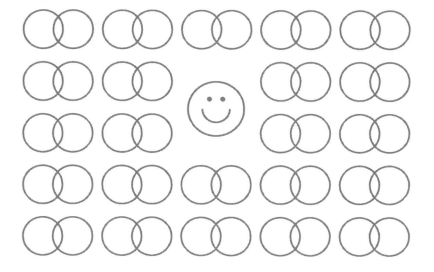

CHAPTER 4

Prepare your Action Plan

So, hopefully, you now have some SMART goals for what you want to achieve in a given timescale. Actually, you may have only one clear SMART goal but that is enough for you to move on to this section. Whether you have just one or many goals, you are committed to taking some action to *expand your life*. Each and every goal now needs an Action Plan. Through the advice in this section, based on my own experiences, I am going to help you to build as many Action Plans as you need for the goals you have.

But before going any further, I recommend that you concentrate on one goal and the development of one Action Plan at a time. Don't overcomplicate things. Keep it simple. This will concentrate your mind and efforts. I will do the same and refer only to a goal or a Plan in the singular rather than the plural throughout this section.

The first thing that I would like you to do is to imagine that your SMART goal requires you to undertake a journey in order to succeed. Every type of activity that we have looked at so far requires you to go somewhere in order to achieve it. Even if you can do everything else online, you have to walk through a door at the end of a journey: the door into a café, the pub, the cinema, the gym, the rehearsal space, the charity shop where you are volunteering. The journey is **how** you achieve your goal! To help you, I am going to guide you through how to plan thoroughly so that you can carry out your goal with total confidence and, ultimately, total success.

I know that you will have regularly undertaken the activity in your goal with at least one other person or a group of friends or family. You may even have been the person who regularly organised everything to do with trips, visits or jaunts. But this time you will not be meeting someone there, or being picked up and given a lift, or joining a group in the place you go to every Friday night. You will still do all those things with other people. But for this goal to be met, you will be on your own the whole time. And you have chosen to achieve this goal so that you are not always waiting to be invited, asked along to make up numbers, or missing out on something because no one else among your friends or family is interested in going with you.

So, please remember that the advice I am giving here has been compiled to help someone – you – who is not only trying to overcome the fear of feeling *visibly alone* but also:

- Has never undertaken the activity in question on their own and/or:

- Is nervous and lacks confidence about undertaking that activity.

I expect that at least some people might want to know exactly what an Action Plan looks like. Well, it is basically a template that covers all the things that you need to decide, do, have in place, to make sure that you can achieve your goal. For every component part of your goal, what are the actions that you must complete, in what order and by when? At its simplest, it is the ultimate tick list that must meet your specific needs!

Here is a simple Plan that I have drawn up below and which you can modify to suit your needs. For this example, I have taken one of the SMART goals included in Chapter 2.

Goal	I will go and see the new James Bond film on the first Saturday of showing at a local cinema, when it opens in June.
Date	The specific Saturday in June.
Cinema choices	Is there more than one local cinema that you could attend? Which is the closest/largest/most comfortable etc? Be sure to take account of the points that matter most to you.
Film showing times	These may also impact on your choice of cinema. So, list the showing times for each cinema you are considering. Which programme fits in best with what you are doing that day? For example, do you need to have a meal beforehand? Are public transport times a consideration?
Ticket	This covers both buying and collecting. Are tickets cheaper at one cinema compared to another? Can you get discounts/concessions for students or seniors as appropriate? Can you choose the best purchase and collection methods to suit you? Can you even choose your ticket collection method?
Transport	How are you going to get there and back safely? Will you need to drive or is public transport an option? Is public transport the only option?
Your choices	Roxy cinema in town; 4.30pm showing; pick up ticket at cinema in advance the day before; bus there, taxi back.
Tick list	• Showing times by cinema • Collect ticket • Bus times and ticket price • Film programme end (for taxi time) • Book taxi home

Now, to ensure that you will have everything you need for every step of your journey, your advance preparation and planning will need to cover, specifically:

- Activity specific details.

- Deciding the best travel arrangements for you.

- How to avoid surprises at the end of the journey.

Activity specific details

For example, the venue, date, the best time to go. Whether to book seats, buy tickets, make reservations as appropriate. To help you to make the choices that suit you best, I have compiled all my best tips and advice, gathered over many years, which have been extensively tried and tested. You will get the benefit of my experiences, including from the mistakes I made and subsequently put right. And to make it easy for you to home in on your own specific goal, I have attributed the tips and advice to specific activities, or a group of activities, where the same or similar advice applies. But some tips may also be helpful for other activities as they are not mutually exclusive.

This advice compilation is in Chapter 5: Activity-related advice, for ease of reference. I hope you will find it helpful both psychologically, particularly in relation to why you should try to strike out on your own, and practically. In short, why you should and how you can *expand your shrunken life*.

Travel arrangements

What's the issue here? I can imagine you thinking you just get in the car/go by tube or bus as you always do wherever you are going.

But for some people these aren't always viable options and they may have other considerations – for example, safety if travelling after dark.

I haven't always been a driver and owned a car. When I lived in London on my own, and without a car-driving partner, I travelled everywhere by tube or bus, whichever was the most convenient for getting from A to B. When I last lived in Sheffield, I could travel by bus or tram, or walk as I did to work every day. Now, having become a driver in mid-life, and having also retired, I drive or walk everywhere in my local vicinity. But recently, having moved to a different part of the same town, I am now having to reassess my previous walking habits. For example, I used to live a five-minute walk away from my local cinema, a close friend, my local pub and my beautician; a ten-minute walk away from the centre of town, the heart of the shopping centre and my hairdresser. I can still walk to all of these places and see all of these people but each is a longer and more time-consuming journey, the result being that I might need to consider transport, at least for the return journey.

Any return journey needs to take account of so many considerations: for example, the time of day, whether you might be drinking alcohol, the safety of certain routes after dark and distance from home. Although a walk into town during daylight hours from my new location is perfectly OK, walking home after dark is a different issue altogether. The main issue is the lack of street lighting, particularly along roads that skirt canals or cross housing or industrial estates. I am not judging local authorities for making cost-saving decisions about street lighting. I am merely pointing out that these decisions have an impact on the choices that women, in particular, have to make about how they travel around their home town/location after dark.

Taking these into account, and to maintain my social life, I now need to know bus numbers and times at certain stops, and the phone numbers and taxi rank locations of local taxi companies in and around town. Taxis can be expensive, especially if travelling relatively late at night. Do you know the cost of a cab from the venue to your home at different times of the day or night? You can find out by phoning the taxi company. It will be worth knowing whether or not a cab is too expensive, or exactly how much change you need in your purse/pocket to pay for a cab at the end of an evening.

For many people, public transport may be the only way to afford to travel around town. So you need to know bus/tram/tube/train lines, any changes and the appropriate stops you need to get there and back. Plus the cost for a single/return/season or senior ticket. All need to be investigated.

For each goal, your Plan needs to show how you are going to get there and how you are going to get back home again safely, and an estimated cost of your transport, in sufficient detail. You won't be able to rely on someone else to organise the arrangements for you. And you don't want to miss out by missing the last bus. So, get on with it.

Avoiding surprises

If you have been to the venue in question many times before, you probably won't need to be reminded about where the different entrances are for ticket seating (for example, stalls, circle, members), the location of the loos, the bars on different floors for different ticket holders, where to get a programme or details of up-coming events. But if you have never been before, you need to know all these things in advance.

When you go somewhere with a friend who has been to the place before, he/she will be able to tell you where to go if, for example, you need the loo. If you go somewhere with a friend and neither of you have been there before, you can help each other and find out together.

'Oh, look! I can see the Ladies/ Gents sign over there.'

'It looks like the ushers are selling programmes on the way into the auditorium.'

And have you noticed that if you are with a friend, how much easier it is to ask other people for help and information than when you are on your own? Funny that.

You want everything to go smoothly at your venue of choice. You want to feel comfortable in your surroundings, not out of place. You want to look and feel as if you know where you are going once you are inside. As if you are moving instinctively to collect your ticket or order a drink at the bar. All of this will not only make you feel confident but you will also appear to be confident to those around you, and those who are serving you. So, if you have never been before, or you have only ever been when you failed to pay attention, then you need to do an advance recce. This means going for a trial run that covers everything except the actual event (film, play, match etc.) included in your goal. And with the information that you need at your fingertips, it will be so much easier to forget about that stupid helmet that you used to wear!

What you need to concentrate on are the details about what it might be like when you get there. You don't want any surprises. If you are driving, where do you park and how much does it cost? Check all routes and entrance locations. Which is the most popular/ busy? What is the best time to get there? What are the queues like? Are there separate queues for people buying or collecting pre-paid tickets? Where do people stand when they've collected their ticket? Do they go straight into the theatre/cinema/event? Is there a long walk or stair climb to get to your seat? Are there lifts if you need to take one? Where is the bar? How do you order an interval drink, if there is an interval? Is there a cloakroom and do you have to pay? How much? Where are the loos?

On the subject of loos, it can't be right that we women have grown accustomed to the shortage of ladies' toilets in any building constructed before around 1990. We shouldn't have to tackle this by trying to avoid going to the loo in a public building for entertainment, for example by emptying our bladder beforehand, at a different location. So ladies, be prepared to go into the Gents – nine times out of ten there is nobody in there. Form a queue – for the Gents. Only let men who claim to be desperate for a wee go in front of a woman in the queue. This is the way changes in society are made.

Back to avoiding surprises, let's look at any additional costs. The most likely culprits here are refreshments and a programme. Ask yourself if you really need a souvenir programme. If you know that you will want to buy one, know how much you will need to pay. Regarding refreshments, unless you are at a local venue run and subsidised by membership fees, prices are jaw-droppingly high. I'm not advocating that you take along some home-made sandwiches and gin and tonic in a small plastic bottle (if your luck is anything like mine, you would have these confiscated during a security check). I'm just advising that you need to be prepared to pay the price or to resist. I never buy refreshments in the large chain cinemas, for example, because I've seen the same bags of sweets and chocolates for sale in Poundland. I try to eat beforehand or know that I will be eating soon after returning home.

Remember that in putting together your Plan you will need to take into consideration some of the things, such as a change of location, that I talked about in Chapter 3, in connection with conquering your fear of being *visibly alone*. You will also need to look at the specific tips and advice I give you in Chapter 5. Plus anything else that is to do with your own considerations and issues that I couldn't possibly know about! Believe me, it is worth taking the trouble to delve into this level of detail, at least while planning your first few steps to fulfilling a solo goal. Once you have got the idea about the things that you need to take into account for you to do something successfully on your own, you won't need anything more than the final tick list. Ask yourself if you have everything you need to do it successfully. By successfully, I mean having fun going to an event/ undertaking an activity on your own without any hitches.

For your goal achievement, concentrate on what you might have to do to find out all the things that will make a difference to your comfort and peace of mind on the day. You don't just want to tick off achievement of a goal, you want to be able to have achieved it well. With bells and whistles would be even better! The following exercise can be done before you have attempted an advance recce, as it could help you to find the important questions that you need to answer in order to complete your Plan. Alternatively, you can do it after you have already done a recce and your Plan appears to be complete. That way you will be in a better position to imagine yourself fulfilling your goal at the actual location, and you may see something that you realise you have overlooked. You can, of course, undertake the exercise both before and after a venue recce, if you feel that is required.

EXERCISE 4

As with Exercise 1, I recommend that you allocate some special time for yourself, at home. You can do this in the daytime or in the evening, as long as you can make sure that you will have no distractions. So switch off your TV and mobile phone. Unplug your landline. Set the mood with dim lighting, gentle music and by lighting a scented candle. Make yourself comfortable, either seated or lying down, perhaps putting a cushion behind your head and one under the backs of your knees. Snuggle under a blanket if you need to feel cosy and warm. Take as long as you need to get ready and settle down for some quiet you-time.

This exercise has four stages. At each stage, first read the scenario and questions I have provided. Then apply the scenario to your own goal, so that it is specific to your anticipated, successful experience. You can put in as much detail as you like. If you imagine that something is going wrong during any of the stages, this will remind you that you need to ensure you take account of this possibility in your Plan.

Stage 1: Imagine that it is the day when you are going to fulfil your goal. How are you feeling? Nervous? Excited? A bit of both? You are checking that you have everything you need for your trip. What are those things? Tickets for entrance and/or travel? Directions? Money for a programme, an ice-cream and the cab fare home? Gloves and a large scarf in case it is chilly later? List them mentally, find them and tick them off your imaginary list.

Stage 2: Now you are on the way there. What time of the day is it? How are you travelling? In your car? Are you listening to music? On the bus? Or the train? Are you running to schedule? Are there hold-ups or delays? How are you coping with the journey? Are you relaxed because you know you have enough time because you set off early? Imagine your journey and how you feel as you get closer to, and finally arrive at, your travel destination. Is this the venue, or do you need to travel further to get to it? Do you know how to get there? Imagine parking the car/stepping off the bus or train and finishing your journey to the venue with ease, as you have planned.

Stage 3: You arrive at the venue. Are you in good time? Early? A bit later than you hoped? How do you feel about that? What is the atmosphere like at the venue? What can you hear and smell? Do people appear to be excited? Are you? What do you need to do next or before the event starts? Put your coat in the cloakroom? Collect a pre-paid ticket? Go to the loo? Order an interval drink? All of those things? Imagine doing the things that you need to do for your goal. Do you know where to go in the venue? Do you need to ask for directions/help? Or is it all just as when you did your recce visit? Imagine walking through to your seat. Taking your seat and settling yourself in for the entertainment. Feel that moment of anticipation.

Stage 4: It is over. The event was everything that you hoped it would be – and more. Feel your joy and see yourself smiling happily. Do you exchange a few words with any of the people around you? What do you say? Do you need to collect your coat? Go to the loo? Imagine yourself walking through the foyer to the street outside and feeling the cold air/the sun on your face/a light drizzle. How do you feel about what you have just experienced? Imagine yourself thinking about that as you make your way to where your car is parked or the bus stop/train station. Now imagine a smooth journey home via your chosen mode of transport. Think especially about how it feels to have achieved your goal. How pleased and proud of yourself you are. How you might celebrate. What you will tell your friends and family about your trip. When you will do the same, or something similar, again.

Remember to try to achieve only one goal at a time, and to prepare an Action Plan in respect of each goal. Don't forget to look at the activity-related advice in Chapter 5. This will hopefully help you to think through options available, deciding factors and the detail that is relevant to your goal. As you start to prepare your Plan for your chosen goal, you may decide to go through the above exercise more than once, both before and after you have undertaken a venue recce, if you think that once is not enough.

By now, you will have at least one SMART goal to fulfil and an Action Plan to help you to achieve it. You have bought a ticket, if one is needed, you know how you are going to get there and back and how much it is likely to cost you in total, including extras. You've checked out the venue and imagined being there and achieving your goal. So, what next? Proceed to Chapter 6.

CHAPTER 5

Activity-related advice

1. Dining out

If you are intent on making a real change that will impact on the quality of your life alone, then being able to stop and order a drink or a bite to eat wherever you are in the world including, most importantly, your local high street, is top of my list.

By dining out I mean anything that involves eating and/or drinking on your own, in a public restaurant, café, bistro, pub, diner, wine bar, coffee shop etc., out of choice. Now, I can hear you saying, 'Why on earth would I want to do that? I'd have no one to talk to.' I know people for whom one or maybe two of the dining experiences in the above list hold no fear and they do them regularly. For example, those who stop off for a coffee at the same café on their way home from the gym or visiting a relative. Or those, predominantly men, who call in regularly for a drink at the same pub on their way home from work. Or people who, after teaching a voluntary class like me, or playing the church organ at the weekend, treat themselves to lunch in a local restaurant.

The reason why I and other people are able to do these things is that we have made these activities a part of our routine. We have woven them into the fabric of our lives. And we are helped in doing them regularly by the people who serve us, recognise us, ask how we are and generally make us feel welcome. Importantly, the reason why those who serve us do this, is because we have managed to cultivate their idea of us as regular customers whom they value: we go to their café, pub, bistro on our own sometimes every Saturday, sometimes a few times a week, maybe once a month. Even better than that, I find that the people who own and work in a place that you frequent feel that they know you better, and therefore serve you better, if they are used to seeing you both in a group and on your own.

So, if you are looking for a place in which to eat or drink alone for the very first time, choose one that you have been to before with someone else, or a group of friends. There are so many places these days that are open all day (or almost all day) serving everything from breakfast to late night supper, tea and coffee, non-alcoholic and alcoholic drinks. If you are lucky enough to have a place nearby that fulfils that list, you will rarely need to go anywhere else. But wherever you choose, make sure that it is somewhere where you will feel comfortable and there is a choice of different seating. Remember Chapter 4? You won't get any unwanted surprises and you can avoid a venue recce. However, don't choose one where you are likely to bump into someone you don't want to see, for example an ex-spouse.

Alternatively, if you don't want to be too adventurous for your first solo outing, you could try the supermarket café after you have finished your shopping. You may have to do a bit of informal research to spot the least busy service times, and if the ambience is not one in which you would want to loiter, you will at least have something in common with the other customers.

Whilst I can't guarantee the quality of the food and drink, here are my top tips for a stress-free solo dining-out experience.

- Don't book in advance for a table for one. You might have noted that you are planning to go there in your diary (a commitment!), or planned in your head to go there, but you don't need to tell the venue. You are on your way to or from somewhere or something and can't guarantee the time you will arrive anyway. Or you could be just walking past. Remember, this event is fitting around other things going on in your day, fitting in with your lifestyle. You never book unless for a gourmet tasting evening – and who goes to those?

- Avoid the busiest times of day when eating out, especially peak lunch service times (until, that is, you become a valued customer). There is nothing more soul destroying than having a waiter shout 'Table for one!' at the top of his voice in a restaurant heaving with people, and being led through them to a rickety table in a dimly lit alcove. You want to be able to choose your table, if possible, so go when there are likely to be tables free. Make a point of telling the waiter that you need some light to be able to read (see below) or to be near a window. Don't be afraid to turn down a first offering and to select another table that you prefer. In time, a good waiter who values your regular custom will always offer you your favourite table, and even reserve it for you.

- It goes without saying that you should be polite and charming to everyone who is serving you, and tip as appropriate. But don't overdo do it. Avoid being ingratiating and smarmy. Remember you want to be welcomed and valued.

- Take something with you to read or do: a book, a magazine, the crossword, some sketching, notes for something you are writing (they might think you are a reviewer or critic). The last thing you want is to be sitting alone at a table with nothing to do but stare around at all the other customers. You are a busy person, you need a break and you've stopped by at this particular place for refreshment and you've brought something along to help you relax and/or occupy your mind. Taking something familiar with you will also help you to feel more at ease in your surroundings.

- Take something with you that either is work or implies that you are working: your phone, tablet or laptop. Even if you are merely working through and deleting your unread emails, or checking Facebook, you appear to be busy. But you are not so busy that you haven't got good manners and forget to be charming and polite – see above. Try to avoid an increasing tendency in recent years for customers to stay for four hours and drink only one black coffee. It will not endear you to the owner and staff who won't necessarily welcome you with open arms again. Remember, you want to be a valued customer.

- Never, if you are a woman, go out for a drink alone at night. But an exception might be to call into your friendly local for a nightcap on the way home. In order for it to become your friendly local, you will perhaps already be a regular customer, either alone or as part of a group, at other times of the day or week. Or you will have gone into it alone for the first time at some point. When I moved house, I did this when I was walking home from a rehearsal one weekday night. I had my script with me, so I had something to read, and sat at the bar. It was a quiet night and the barman chatted with me about the play. I left after one drink but went back a few weeks later on a different night at an earlier time, and another time I took a friend there. And now I can go in and feel comfortable there anytime I like. As a valued customer.

- My preferences for eating out are breakfast, brunch or a late lunch. A few years ago, I used to prepare my teaching notes for the class I was about to give whilst having breakfast at a café in town. Later on, I started to treat myself to a lunch out after teaching the class. Now, I'm a fan of the mid-morning to pre-lunch timing of the brunch, especially at the weekend when I can take a broadsheet newspaper and have some quality me-time.

If you have never before tried this most liberating of experiences, I promise you that you will be safe, and have fun, if you follow my advice. Not only that, if you succeed you will feel properly grown up – and want to do it again.

2. Going to the cinema

Now you've just started to read this and you're already wondering why on earth you would even consider going to see a film on your own at the actual cinema. You'll have nobody next to you to nudge during a funny bit, share popcorn with, pass you a hankie or chat with afterwards. Plus you could just wait for it to come out on DVD. Well, I don't need someone with me to fall about laughing in the aisles (see my choice of seat below), cry buckets of tears at a weepie, jump out of my seat in fear or shock, or eat most of the popcorn. Neither do you if you think about it. And there's nothing like seeing a film ahead of your friends and/or colleagues and telling them about it – even better, recommending that they go and see it. Remember, you are free to go to see a film when it suits you. Most of them will probably need to liaise with a significant other.

- Choose the film you want to see and then check where and when it is showing at local cinemas near you. The websites for local cinemas will have full programme listings and film showing times. The dates and times of film showings may vary by venue, and a choice of venue and times is useful. I always write down all dates and times for each cinema in my local area so that I know all my options. You can't assume that if the film you want to see is being screened at 6pm on a Tuesday it will be screened at the same time on another day at the same cinema.

- Choose a day and screening time that fits around you and your lifestyle. That fits in with what else you are doing on a particular day. For example, if you regularly shop in town or have an appointment near to the cinema on a certain day, plan to fit in around that. A good film after the chore of a supermarket shop or a dental or business appointment is a fitting reward. Alternatively, you may only be free to see your chosen film on one particular day so your choices are limited.

- I prefer to go to an afternoon or early evening screening if I am on my own. These times of the day are less busy and there is more chance of being able to get a ticket without having to book in advance. There is also the added advantage, if needed, of being less *visibly on your own* during these quieter business periods, even on the busiest days of the week and weekends.

- Check if there are any ticket price discounts, for example:

  - On a specific day of the week. At my local cinema all ticket prices for all films and screenings are reduced on a Tuesday.

  - For specific groups, for example students of any age (with a current student institution identity card); or seniors (usually aged 60 or over with age verification such as a driving licence). My local cinema has a 'Silver Screening' for seniors every Monday with a reduced price ticket and free cup of tea or coffee with biscuits.

- Buy your ticket in advance if you want the best available seat or a seat in your preferred position. I always try to get an aisle seat to avoid squeezing past people when getting in and out of the row. It is also useful to slip into just before the film starts and to slip out of if I need to go to the loo, without drawing attention to myself.

- Tickets are available to buy online, at a ticket dispensing machine in the foyer, via a telephone booking line and in person at a booking/ticket sales booth or general-purpose counter. Note that telephone booking lines are invariably and infuriatingly automated so you will need your wits, your credit or debit card and a swear box handy if you go down this route. If, like me, you want to guarantee your seat of choice, and speak to an actual salesperson, go to the cinema and buy your ticket in person. This can be done in advance and presents a number of additional advantages (see Chapter 4).

- If you would prefer to see a film with a group of film fans, or as a member of a film club, the cinema may be able to give you information about any in your area. If not, try local online information such as your 'Streetwise' site.

Why not check your local cinema listings right now?

3. Going to see a live show performance

By a show, I mean any live performance at a theatre, which could include a play, a musical, an opera, a concert by an orchestra, musician, singer, band or choir, a dance spectacular, or a performance by a magician, a hypnotist, comedian(s) or a celebrity speaker. So, every time I say 'show', I am using the term generically.

By a theatre, I mean not only a traditional or purpose-built theatre or arena, but also any building that is being used as a general-purpose space in order to stage a show or other performance event, for example a disused and converted factory, church or bank. I am therefore also using the word 'theatre' as a generic term.

If you have never been to a theatre to see a show, and don't ever intend to as it is not up your street, I recommend that you give this section a read. You might find a night out at a show is a much more attractive prospect than you imagined. Especially if the alternative is sitting at home alone, thinking about your *shrunken life*, and there is nothing on the telly. For a start, every performance is live and therefore unique. Plus, all theatres have a bar and you can even take alcoholic drinks (in plastic containers) into the auditorium these days, for some shows.

If you have been used to going to shows with a partner or someone else who is no longer around, there is no reason to deprive yourself. Why miss out on seeing the latest hit shows or musicals? Or seeing a big Hollywood star debut in the West End? Or the latest TV magician, your favourite comedian's new stand-up routine, a band you admire, a neighbour, relative or friend on stage for the first time? Remember, the people sitting around you will also be fans or enthusiasts so you will have something in common with them and something to talk about. Why *shrink your life* to exclude the joy that a trip to the theatre gives you? You don't have to.

For many people, going to see a show means a trip to the London West End. However, ticket prices are now so expensive that only hedge fund managers and foreign tourists can afford to buy them. In addition, for anyone who is further than a daytrip away from London, seeing a show involves staying overnight with all the additional expense that incurs. London hotels are among the most expensive in the world, especially if you want a room for sole occupancy – like we do! So, a London show is an expensive treat for a special occasion.

Here are my show-stopping tips.

- For any show, anywhere, that you definitely want to see, buy a ticket in advance:

    - Preview tickets for West End, the National and Royal Shakespeare Theatres, and most regional theatres, are offered at a discount. Previews are like dress rehearsals before a show officially opens and has been reviewed by the press critics. Technical difficulties may arise but that is the reason for the discount.

    - Become a member of a theatre to get advance programme details and discounted ticket offers for one or more shows where the tickets are bought together. Advance ticket sales to members often account for tickets being sold out before a show opens.

    - Phone the box office to see if any unbought, spare single seats are available. They will love you for wanting to take one off their hands, especially if it is in the middle of a row in the stalls. You will love them if it is anywhere in the stalls without a restricted view.

- Whenever I can, I prefer to go to a matinée performance. This is because most evening shows don't end until 10pm or even later. I don't want to be out too late at night, going home on my own, especially if I have travelled to London for a production. Most professional theatres have two matinée performances a week, one on a selected weekday (check listings) and one on a Saturday. Matinée performance tickets are sometimes cheaper than those for an evening performance.

- Tickets for shows on the day aren't normally available for the casual passer-by, but:

  - Some theatres, such as the National and Royal Shakespeare Theatres and regional theatres have a limited number of tickets available to buy on the day, for sale from 10am. You normally have to queue and some tickets might be for standing or restricted view only.

  - The Society of West End Theatres ticket booth in London's Leicester Square offers discounted matinée and evening performance tickets for a limited number of shows each day. Don't expect to get a seat for the most popular shows but you can see a great show you've never heard of at a bargain price.

  - Other ticket agencies around the West End might advertise ticket availability for popular or supposedly sold-out shows. But ticket prices are likely to be marked up rather than down.

- Support your local and/or regional professional theatres, where you can:

  - See touring productions of popular West End shows at a fraction of the price.

  - See one-man touring shows by well-known and popular speakers and comedians. My local theatre has a popular comedy festival every October with performances every night for two weeks by new and well-known performers.

— Buy tickets more cheaply than in London plus discounted tickets if you buy for more than one show at a time.

— Join a local theatre supporters' group that arranges visits to certain shows of interest.

— Join a community theatre group and potentially benefit from free theatre workshops and free tickets to certain shows.

- It is also possible to watch live theatre at your local cinema. Nowadays, 'event cinema' as it is called is one of the best and the cheapest way to see a live theatre/opera/ballet performance on the actual night it is staged. In the last few years the National and Royal Shakespeare Theatres, the Royal Opera House, The Globe Theatre, The Barbican and West End theatres have all broadcast simultaneous live performances to cinemas not just across the UK, but across the world. Tickets are individually priced by the theatre for each performance. At the time of writing, the most I have paid has been £12. I highly recommend such events, and they are popular so get tickets well in advance (see the section on the cinema in this chapter).

Don't overlook your local non-professional theatre groups as a means of enjoying theatre produced and performed by local people for local people. There is bound to be at least one group operating in your vicinity. They actively encourage membership, which usually brings with it ticket price and other discounts. In my experience, theatre groups are friendly and clubbable and never let anyone sit or stand *on their own* in a corner for long.

4. Going for a walk

Research evidence from around the world shows overwhelmingly that being outdoors, surrounded by the natural landscape, is not just good for us, it is vital for our wellbeing at every age. Trees and plants emit phytoncides which, when inhaled, slow down breathing and reduce anxiety. Negative ions that proliferate alongside lakes and riverbanks are natural antidepressants. So, a walk through parkland or a forest, especially alongside or around water, can reduce stress and blood pressure, and generally impact positively on our emotional and mental health.

Although walking activity for pleasure and improved health has become increasingly popular in recent times, many people feel self-conscious or anxious about striding out alone, especially if they are used to, and have fond memories of, walking with a loved one. Or they think of a walk as something that you always do with someone else, or a group.

By walking for pleasure, I'm talking about walking for exercise and to check in with your natural surroundings. I'm not talking about walking to the shops, which is walking with the purpose of shopping. And I'm not talking about speed walking either, but going at a pace that you feel comfortable with in the environment where you are walking. In addition to pace, the length of the walk or the time you spend on a walk for pleasure is also up to you. A lot of experts have given opinions on the benefits of walking for health in the recent past, but most seem to recommend walking every day for a minimum of 20 minutes continuously (ten minutes in one direction and ten minutes back) to improve or maintain health, especially as we grow older.

I recently started active walking to my gym session and back three times a week. That's 20 minutes each way = 40 minutes a day x three times a week = 120 minutes = two hours of walking for health a week as a minimum. Do you have a similar length journey to a regular appointment to which you could walk rather than drive or take public transport?

SELF-RESPECT 6

We all know about the benefits of regular exercise, don't we? Regular in this context is generally defined as exercise for at least 20 minutes, three times a week. So, based on the recommendations on walking for health above, following these can also more than fulfil requirements for regular exercise, can't they? Not necessarily. If you want to be fit for your Solo Success-full life (see Chapter 2) sign up for a (normally free) assessment with a fitness professional at any local gym. He/she will be able to advise on and devise a personal fitness programme that takes account of any health issues. If you have a known health problem, injury or disability, check with your GP or the health professional who you see regularly, for advice about what type and level of exercise will be appropriate for you.

Value yourself by valuing your fitness.

This is one of the most challenging areas to tackle, given our fear of being *visibly alone*. I have often thought that it is strange in these modern times that people perceive it to be peculiar to go for a solitary walk. More than that, they think it is strange to see people who are on a walk on their own. Yet people go off for walks alone all the time in novels, on TV and in poems: 'I wandered lonely as a cloud...' Moreover, no one ever comments about solitary runners who are pounding the pavements and country lanes.

Of course, you are never alone walking a dog, both in terms of having your pet with you and in terms of the other dog-owners you meet regularly or along the way. So, if you are a dog-owner, that's great. But if not, is the answer then to get a dog? For some people this might be exactly the right thing to do. However, for many this will be out of the question, perhaps because of an illness or allergy, but the most common reason is likely to be housing pet restrictions. However, it may be possible for you to borrow someone else's dog by becoming a volunteer dog walker. Many dog-owners need temporary or more long-term help because of new and difficult circumstances that are dog-unfriendly, such as illness or changes in working hours. If this is something you would like to pursue, look for advertisements in local newspapers or shops, on community noticeboards and on Streetwise online.

If, like so many of us, you are walking without a doggy companion, I have devised some tips to help you to overcome your fears and build up your confidence to walk alone happily, safely and without attracting attention to yourself.

- Never go out alone at night. Only people who live in the TV world of *Midsomer Murders* do that sort of thing, and we know what always happens to them!

- If you need to have something with you that makes you feel safe, carry a dog lead in your hand. Other people will assume you have a dog nearby. Be prepared, however, to be asked about your dog.

- Don't carry a handbag. You are not going visiting or to the shops. You might need to carry essentials such as money, house keys, mints, tissues. I don't class a phone as essential, unless I might want to use the camera, but I accept that you might want or need to have your phone with you. I suggest that you carry a small rucksack/backpack or wear a bum-bag. Or, do as I do these days and put all my essentials in zipped pockets in my coat, jacket or trousers.

- Dress the part. Take a tip from the runners who wear appropriate clothing and footwear for their activity that, interestingly, blends into the urban landscape. You can buy specialist activity wear, such as tops, trousers and jackets that are weather and/or sweat sensitive, if you think that is necessary. But I don't mean for you to go out and buy a lot of new, specialist clothing. No, I'm talking about the things we all have, like a pair of trainers or walking shoes, a waterproof or showerproof anorak or cagoule. In summer, you can carry a showerproof jacket and a sweatshirt in your rucksack/backpack in case the weather turns chilly.

- Always carry a small bottle of water with you in your rucksack/backpack or bum-bag (my bum-bag has a special Velcro fastened loop to hold a bottle of water). If you don't feel up to stopping for a drink at a café (that might be a quite different goal) carrying a bottle of water is the next best thing.

- If you need an additional distraction, listen to your favourite music or the spoken word played on a portable device through headphones. I know people who listen to audio books, the radio and catch up with their favourite shows via digital services whilst out walking. Although this cuts out any traffic noise in an urban environment, please be mindful of your safety and the safety of others if you wear headphones. I have to say that when in the country I think it is a shame to cut out the sound of birdsong.

- If, as discussed in Chapter 3, you want to avoid being *visibly alone* in your local area, you could drive to a different location, such as a well-known beauty spot. You might be surrounded by other people who are also enjoying the walk and the sights, but you are less likely to bump into someone you know. And if you observe the dress codes above, you won't stand out.

- Walk purposefully. Look as if you know where you are going. I have been the butt of jokes all my life because of the way I have always walked swiftly to get where I am going – or scooted along, sped as if on skates or casters according to reports. I'm not so fast now! But you don't have to move quickly to move with purpose and intent. Hold your chin up so that you can see where you are going. Relax your shoulders down and breathe evenly. Let your breathing and your stride develop an easy, steady rhythm. And smile. People you see will smile back at you.

If you want to continue walking for pleasure but decide you don't want to do this alone, the best thing is to join a local walking group, for example through the Ramblers' Association. You will be able to find details of all local groups, and all other walking groups that have a website, via the internet.

When I retired a few years ago, I knew that I would miss being surrounded by my colleagues throughout the day. So, I followed up a recommendation to join a daytime walking group and took a course in active walking with two objectives: to get fit after doing a sedentary office job for years and to make sure that at some points in the week I would be around other people with a shared interest. I made some very good friends and took up other activities as a result. Although I no longer belong to the original group, I'm still an active walker and practise the technique regularly on my own, around the park, riverside and canal walks of my local town. I can do it on my own because I learned the value of all the above tips and advice.

CHAPTER 6

Put the plan into action

OK. Now it is show-time! You are going to do it. You are going to achieve your goal. You are going to do it because you know all these things:

WHEN? You have an actual date and time. They are in your SMART goal.

WHERE? You are familiar with the venue. It holds no surprises for you.

WHAT? You are going to do something that you want to do on your own: watch/do/take part in something – an event, something special or even mundane.

HOW? You know exactly how you will get there and back and how much it is likely to cost you. Plus, you followed an Action Plan of your own devising. That's how.

WHY? Because **you want to** *expand your shrunken solo life.* You want to be able to do things without relying on other people to do them with you. You no longer wear that stupid helmet! Because you want to be a Solo Success!

If all the above is true, then you have no excuses. If it is not true, then you need to go back over the earlier chapters to see what you have missed out or forgotten, or still need to work on. Chucking that stupid helmet in the skip, perhaps? Go back to Exercise 3.

I'll come clean here, and tell you that I wouldn't have been able to say everything in that list was true for some of the things that I attempted for the first time on my own. I wish that I had gone to the lengths of such meticulous planning beforehand many a time. I have included a few of my own clangers that resulted in failure in the Table on pages 91 and 92. But it is because of the mistakes I made, and what I learned as a result, that I'm able to advise you in this way. My failures will hopefully lead to your successes!

So, I'm going to assume that the above list is all true and you have no excuse anymore not to fulfil your goal. I know that you are likely to feel a mixture of nerves and excitement, increasingly as the day approaches. Alternatively, you may have pushed it to the back of your mind, trying to forget about it, not wanting to dwell on it too much in case you change your mind and chicken out. Either way, here are the three big secrets I know that will help to strengthen your resolve to follow through.

SECRET 1: Put the event in your diary! A diary in any format, traditional paper or digital, such as on your phone or tablet. It needs to be the one that you use regularly. Or write it on your To-do list. Or even on a scrap of paper stuck to your fridge under a magnet depicting a Swiss cuckoo clock. Whatever you do, just write it down somewhere where you will see it regularly. In this way, you are making a commitment. It is in your diary, so you will be committed to doing it. If someone asks you if you are free on the date and around the time that you are committed to fulfilling your goal, you are not free. You must apologise to that person. 'Sorry, but I'm going to [insert details].' This leads me neatly into the next secret.

SECRET 2: Tell other people your plans! Not random people in the street but people you know – your family and friends or colleagues. Or acquaintances with whom you might pass the time of day at the places that you go to with other people: work, the gym, church for example. If someone asks what you are doing on THE DAY – tell them. Or you might introduce it yourself, casually, for example: 'I'm going to see the new James Bond film at the weekend.' Not too much detail, notice. You don't need to bare your soul unless, of course, you want to. The more that you tell people what you are going to do and when, the more confident you will become about fulfilling your goal, and the more you will believe that you will do it.

I teach a drama class on Saturday morning at a local theatre in a nearby city. As the class finishes at lunchtime I am usually ready for something to eat straight afterwards. Driving to my class, I usually decide which local café or bistro I fancy having something to eat in that lunchtime. However, I always know that on the drive back home I could change my mind and make myself something to eat at home instead. So if as I am leaving, a colleague asks, "Where are you off to now, Chris?" I tell them where I am planning to go for lunch. And that's it, I feel committed to going there. Fortunately, I have a number of regular Saturday lunchtime spots (see my tips and advice on dining out in Chapter 5).

SECRET 3: Arrange to do something with friends or family on a day shortly after the day of the event. This is so that you have a ready-made support group around you to either congratulate or commiserate with you, depending on the outcome of the event. Whether you think you will have told them about it, or whether you think you will need them or not, this is a good forward planning tactic. Either way, it will be a pleasant distraction that stops you dwelling too much by yourself on success or failure.

Finally, the last piece in the jigsaw of preparation for the BIG DAY. You've prepared yourself mentally and psychologically. Now prepare yourself physically so that you feel and look good, no matter what it is that you are going to do. Decide what you are going to wear, what is the most appropriate for you to wear at the venue, for the event and the time of day. Set it out beforehand. Give yourself time to get ready. Enjoy it and let this help you to feel an excited anticipation for what you are going to achieve.

Go and achieve it.

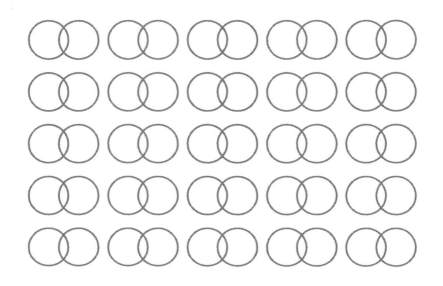

RESULTS

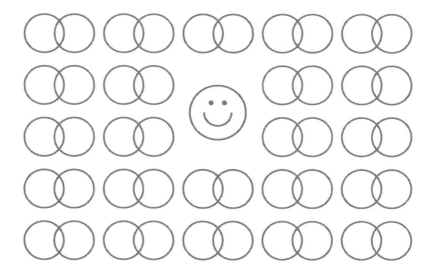

CHAPTER 7

Review the event

So, how did it go? You knew that I would ask!

If you were successful, and you had a good time, and there were no hitches that phased you, EXCELLENT! Well done! Once you have finished with your celebrating, think about **why** you achieved your goal so successfully. The reason that this is so important is because, hopefully, you will identify that it had something to do with the preparation and planning that you undertook. If this is the case, hopefully it means that you will see that it is worth trying the same approach with all the other goals that you want to achieve, through the Action Plans that you will devise and follow.

You may even want to experience the same thing again. In which case, you just need to make a few fine adjustments to your SMART goal and your Action Plan. Until, that is, you don't need them any more, because you will be able to do it all instinctively. Look forward to that day! It will come.

If the outcome was less than totally successful (right up to and including total disaster) then you will need to put a bit of time and effort into working out what went wrong. Not only that, but what, if anything, you can do to make sure that the same thing doesn't happen in the future. However, lest you forget any crucial detail, get down to the analysis of shortcomings straight away. You need to have done this before the meeting you have arranged with family and friends – see **SECRET 3** above – because if you do feel in the mood for sharing anything, you don't want them chipping in with what, for them, passes for advice. You want them to be supportive not destructive. So, you need to have worked out everything beforehand, including the tale you are going to tell. If you don't want to talk about it, there's no problem because, as I said above, this meet-up is a pre-arranged pleasant distraction.

How to go about admitting what went wrong during your event that prevented it from being a 100% success? That might be a case of identifying how many times you felt *visibly alone* and wearing that stupid helmet! Moreover, what can you do to prevent the same or a similar thing happening in the future? Well, to help you out, I've devised a problem disaster-scale to help you not only to identify what went wrong for you, but also how to put that into perspective in terms of fixability in the future.

Once you have absorbed the table below, and I hope that you can see the funny side, especially where it relates to your experience(s), it should be clear to you where you could have diverted disaster. Where, for example, you would not have found yourself wearing that stupid helmet! That's right – by better planning. So, work out what you could have done to improve matters, and promise yourself that you will work on that area, or areas, when you put together another plan for another goal.

CATEGORY	EXAMPLE CAUSE	RESULT	REMEDY
Minor disasters	Transport late/held up/diverted	You were late and missed start.	In future, plan to set off and arrive early.
	Ticket machine at venue out of order.	You had to queue for your pre-paid ticket.	
	Long queue to get into venue.	Anxiety attack	
Random disasters	Sudden tube and bus strike.	You didn't get there.	In such unforeseen cases, where many are affected, events might be re-scheduled for ticket holders, or the ticket price refunded.
	Arson attack at venue.	Venue closed	
	Sudden death of star player.	Match cancelled	
	Gunman running amok in town centre.	You were held behind police barriers.	
Preventable disasters	Event sold out	No show/match for you.	You need to get a ticket in advance and make sure that it is for the day and time that you plan to visit – as per your goal.
	Senior night Tuesday not Thursday.	You had to buy a full-price ticket.	
	Matinée is on Wednesday.	Went home or hung about for a later show.	
	Your sat-nav takes you to the wrong destination.	Did you eventually find the venue? On time?	Pay more attention to the detail of your return journey requirements and, if necessary, do a trial run to avoid upsets and challenges.
	The carpark you choose is 20 mins walk away from venue.	You are late and have to wait to be shown to your seat at an appropriate moment.	
	You wait 30 mins for a return taxi and then can't pay for it.	You get the bus home after waiting another 30 mins at the stop.	

CATEGORY	EXAMPLE CAUSE	RESULT	REMEDY
Preventable disasters	There is no lift to the top tier seating area and you cannot climb the three flights of stairs.	You are found another seat on the ground level but are forced to pay extra for the more expensive, top-price seat.	You can avert such disasters in future by doing an advance recce of the venue. Remember, you don't want any surprises.
	You are late and have to wait to be shown to your seat at an appropriate moment.	You are mortified, disturb all those seated around you and worse, draw attention to yourself.	
	You cannot buy food/a snack.	You have a couple of drinks instead and fall asleep 20 minutes after taking your seat.	
Natural disasters	Flood	You were evacuated for your own safety.	Depending on damage, as for random disaster, or try again when normality returns, or somewhere else.
	Earthquake		
	Meteorite strike		
	Typhoon		
Total disaster	Combination of minor, random or natural disaster with preventable disaster.	Eventful for all the wrong reasons!	Concentrate on what was preventable – see above.

SELF-RESPECT 7

Whenever we are analysing something that has gone wrong in our life we have a natural tendency to judge ourselves harshly, to beat ourselves up. So, be careful of your own feelings and make sure that the first thing you do – before any self-flagellation – is to identify all the aspects of your goal event that went smoothly and exactly to plan. Always recognise the right stuff, the good bits first of all, and give yourself some praise. Remember to be kind to yourself – you are worthy!

Value yourself by valuing everything that you learn from all your experiences.

I often find that a change of location and a breath of fresh air are good for stimulating the problem-solving part of the brain. To work out what you could have been done to improve matters, and have a better experience in the future, I suggest that you get outside for a change of scene and go for a walk to mull things over (see Chapter 5 on the benefits of going for a walk). In this type of situation, I also try to see the funny side and imagine myself telling a friend about the unfortunate incident(s), in a way that makes fun of me and will (hopefully) make us both laugh. If you can work things out in this way, well they say laughter is the best medicine! Take off that stupid helmet and go and feed the ducks!

Regarding that stupid helmet, you may want to try repeating Exercise 3 and reliving your mortification at wearing that stupid helmet at your goal event, exactly as it happened. Then, in the same way as before, imagine coming out of the building, swearing never to wear the helmet again and throwing it disdainfully into a kerbside skip. This may help to exorcise the memory of the real incident.

Now that you know what went wrong and how to put it right in future, you can go out and enjoy yourself with your family or friends on that night out you arranged beforehand – **SECRET 3** remember? And, regardless of the outcome of your goal, or whether you told them what you were planning to do, you may want to tell them about your recent experience anyway. You don't need to make a big thing of it, even if it was totally successful. Just mention it casually, for example:

'I saw the latest James Bond film last Saturday. It was by far the best.'

'I had lunch at that new bistro on Park Street last week. They've got a fantastic menu.'

'I went to London to see the latest David Hockney exhibition on my day off. I had a great day.'

If they ask you about who you went with, just be honest – you don't have to tell them that you followed a plan outlined in a book! Imagine how liberating it will feel to talk about something that you did by yourself! Imagine how you could like it and get used to it. Imagine that!

And if the outcome of your goal was not totally successful, you may well have that aforementioned funny story to recount about whatever scale of disaster befell you. If you can tell that story and laugh about what happened, it will help to dispel any fear of undertaking a similar exercise again. Although you will never repeat the same mistakes again, because you now know how important it is to plan thoroughly.

When you get home, take a look at the list of SMART goals you made. Or, if there are no further goals, the list of activities that you wanted to be able to do by yourself, in order to *expand your shrunken life*. If you have no more goals or activities on your wish list – WELL DONE! You have done everything you set out to do.

However, if there is at least one more goal, or one more activity on your list that you want to be able to do on your own, decide which one you are going to tackle next.

CHAPTER 8

Celebrate Solo Success!

What constitutes progress? I don't think it is just about the final achievement of one of your goals. It is much more than that: it is every step of the way. In Chapter 4 I talked about the achievement of a goal as being a journey. It includes going through the whole process as a valuable means to overcome your fear of being *visibly alone* and to achieve your desired outcome. So, what are the key steps along the progress journey? I think they are:

- Undertaking the appropriate research about the activity, venue, timings etc;

- Setting a SMART goal;

- Formulating an Action Plan that covers, as necessary:

  - Ticketing/access requirements;

  - Return travel arrangements, including a trial run;

  - A venue recce if necessary;

- Putting the event in your diary;

- Telling other people as a means of firming up your commitment;

- Putting the Plan into action on the BIG DAY;

- Reviewing the outcome;

- In the event of less than 100% success, deciding what needs improvement/inclusion for a further attempt or for another similar goal.

Those steps are produced in a logical sequence. But there is no rule that says you should only start telling people what you are planning to do once you have firmed-up a Plan. The minute that you can say 'I am doing/going to [insert location/venue] on [insert date]' you can start mentioning it, and thereby committing to it. So, that would be as soon as you have set your SMART goal.

Every time you complete each of these steps you are progressing and, at the same time, growing in confidence in your ability to complete the remaining steps. Similarly, every time you complete a goal successfully you will be more confident about setting and completing another one on your list. At some point, you may even have more than one goal set and more than one Action Plan at different progress stages. The point is that you need to keep track of your progress and, importantly, to give yourself a reward as each step is achieved. Although, don't go mad leaping in the air and whooping with delight in public, unless you are absolutely sure that the stupid helmet has been consigned to the skip for good!

You will start to notice that you find it easier to set goals that cover the same ground as those that you have achieved successfully before. These goals just become activities that you prepare and plan for quite naturally, instinctively even, and you probably don't have to look at prompts and write everything down. (Well, if you're like me, you might need a short list!) This is serious progress: you are ultimately aiming to make changes whereby activities that you undertake on your own, when you want to do them, become an integral part of your lifestyle and routine. That is what I mean by *expanding your shrunken life*. Therefore, mentally note and congratulate yourself every time you find yourself achieving something on your own that was on a goal list only a matter of weeks or months ago. This might include acknowledging that you, for example:

- Walk into a favourite café and order a coffee to drink while you check your emails;

- Stop off at the local cinema to buy an advance ticket for a screening you are planning to go to next week;

- Go for a walk along the riverbank in the afternoon to check on the seasonal flowering and to see how much the cygnets have grown;

- Find yourself unexpectedly free, so go to a bistro for lunch and you're warmly greeted by the waiters and given the table of your choice.

That all looks like a pretty amazing lifestyle to me! And that doesn't include all the things that you do with your family and friends. So, when you catch yourself being a Solo Success, make sure that you self-congratulate by saying to yourself, 'Well done me! I walked into here, without feeling that I was *visibly alone*. And now look at me. I'm drinking this fragrant coffee/eating this delicious meal/counting the new ducklings/enrolling on this course...!'

I learned to do all those things and have been a solo practitioner over many years. Yet, I can still remember the feeling of thinking that I am *visibly alone* and can still sometimes feel it. But I can shake it off in a moment, and you will learn to do exactly the same purely by successfully practising the art of doing things on your own. In addition, like me, you will also notice that your development and success becomes self-perpetuating. What I mean by that is that you start to reward your success with a further progression also resulting in success. For example, you might reward a solo turn around the park with a coffee afterwards at a café that you have never been into before and then reward that with a glass of beer or wine on the way back from a difficult appointment which you reward the following week with a trip to the new ice-cream parlour... you get the drift.

Whatever you have successfully achieved as a result of working through this book, whether one goal or more, or even just getting to the end resolving to actually set a goal, I am so pleased to have been able to help you in some way.

Just promise me this: as a person living on your own, under whatever circumstances, you will never go back to living a *shrunken life* but will always strive to live an *expanded life*, in the spirt of a true Solo Success!

Perhaps you know other people who live on their own who might benefit from some of the tips and advice I have given. If so, please recommend this book to them, and tell them it will change their lives into Solo Success-full lives!

Statistical references

1. Between 2004 and 2014 the number of one-person households in the UK rose from 7.2 to 7.6 million. In 2014 this represented 28% of all households, the second largest household group after two-person households (35%). Looking at gender, of the 7.6 million one-person households in 2014, 54% contained one woman and 46% one man. However, it is the age-related data that provides the largest change in trends: the number of one-person households in the 45 to 64 age group rose from 1.92 million in 2004 to 2.43 million in 2014 – an increase of 27%. (*Office for National Statistics (ONS) Labour Force Surveys*)

2. Divorce numbers in England and Wales are falling: in 2014 the number of divorces at 111,169 was 3.1% lower than in 2013 and 27% lower compared with a peak in 2003. However, divorce figures are highest for men aged 45 to 49 and women aged 40 to 44. (*ONS Statistical Bulletin: Divorce in England and Wales 2014*)

3. The main cause of this dramatic increase in households of one amongst the mid-life age group is partnership dissolution leading to divorce. (*Living arrangements in mid-life', Dieter Demey, Anne Berrington, Maria Evandrou and Jane Falkingham (2012)*

About the Author

Christine Ingall was born in Gainsborough, Lincolnshire. Initially, she trained to be a teacher and was awarded a B.Ed. from Manchester University. She worked as a civil servant for 35 years, most recently in the development and implementation of policy and programmes, to support the unemployed and unskilled. She never expected to live a single, solo occupant life for more than 30 years, or that it could be so much fun and pass so quickly. Now retired, she lives 'a charmed life' in Leamington Spa, and actively pursues her interest in the theatre through her membership of The Criterion Theatre in Coventry, where she also teaches drama, and her love of singing through her membership of a local branch of The Rock Choir. She is thrilled to have actually finished and published a book at last, and pleasantly surprised that it turned out to be a work of non-fiction. She is currently working on her next book, *Solo Holidays – 10 rules to ensure a great time on your own.*

www.cjiwrites.com
www.cjiwrites.blog
@cjisolo